2 —

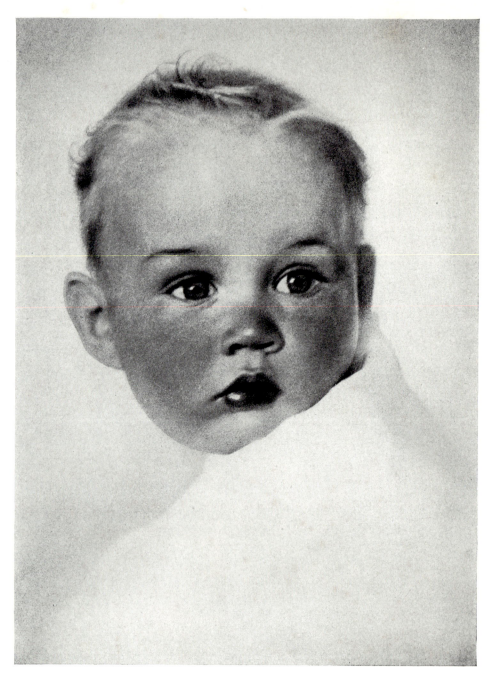

William Mortensen

The New
PROJECTION
CONTROL

by

William Mortensen

CAMERA CRAFT PUBLISHING COMPANY

376 Sutter Street   San Francisco 8, Calif.

Camera Craft Publishing Company

San Francisco

Third Edition
Revised and Enlarged
Second Printing
April, 1944
Third Printing
November, 1945

Other Books by

WILLIAM MORTENSEN

PICTORIAL LIGHTING

MONSTERS AND MADONNAS

THE COMMAND TO LOOK

THE MODEL

PRINT FINISHING

OUTDOOR PORTRAITURE

FLASH IN MODERN PHOTOGRAPHY

Printed in the United States of America
by THE MERCURY PRESS, San Francisco

Contents

Developing procedure. Fixing. Drying and finishing. A point of pride. Two basic technical faults: flatness and excessive contrast. The ultimate photographic test.

Chapter Five—*Local Printing* 50

The unselective camera. The scope of local printing. What the camera sees. A sample of procedure. The tools for local printing. Three types of local printing. Spot printing. Relation of spot printing to general printing. Spot printing for emphasis. Spot printing for elimination. Spot printing for balance. Local printing by cut-outs. Dodging. Dodging to correct unbalanced illumination. Dodging to adjust tonal relationships with background. "Dodging in" for emphasis. Dodging with cut-outs. Dodging in landscape. Vignetting. Vignetting combined with dodging in. The general technique of local printing.

Chapter Six—*Distortion* 86

Art as distortion. The background of distortion. Cultures express themselves through their distortions. The photographic use of distortion. Methods. Samples of procedure. Distortion in landscape. Everyday uses of distortion. Lateral distortion. Local distortion.

Chapter Seven—*Combination Printing* 102

Two types of combination printing. Montage, the combination of ideas. A sample procedure for montage. Technical requirements. Montage in portraiture. Combination of literal elements. Addition of clouds. The use of cut-outs. Variations in procedure. An extreme instance of combination printing.

Chapter Eight—*It's Up to You* 121

The author is slightly depressed. Projection control is readily abused. Projection control is not a means of covering up mistakes. A few last words. The author passes the buck.

Foreword

This volume represents the fourth version of a project that first saw the light of day back in 1933 in the form of a brief magazine article dealing with a few useful tricks in projection printing.

The unexpectedly hearty response to the original article (and its slightly expanded reprint in pamphlet form) revealed that many photographers were intensely interested in exploiting the pictorial possibilities of the projection print and in eluding its sometimes crass limitations. So in 1934, *Projection Control* underwent further growth and blossomed out in book form. It was my first trial at writing a book and was fumbling and tentative in a good many details. Nevertheless, because it offered some suggestions, however incomplete, for making more adequate and imaginative use of the procedure of projection printing, it enjoyed considerable circulation.

Now, once more, *Projection Control* undergoes a metamorphosis This new edition, however, is not a mere revision and expansion of the old. To all intents and purposes, it is a new book, and—I trust—a more useful one.

In general, there is less emphasis on the freakish and "trick" uses of Projection Control, and much fuller consideration of the everyday applications of the procedures involved. Only incidentally is Projection Control a means of contriving startling pictorial effects. Properly understood, it is a method, of everyday usefulness, for making the best possible prints from your negatives.

So I have eliminated most of the material relative to "framing," a subject properly pertaining to composition rather than projection printing. Eliminated also are most of the more *freakish* demonstrations of distortion and multiple printing. In place of these deletions, there is much fuller description of the various procedures, with special emphasis on the applications of Projection Control to ordinary portrait and landscape photography.

WILLIAM MORTENSEN.

Laguna Beach, Calif.
February, 1942

Chapter One

Picture Taking and Picture Making

From its very inception, or at least from the time that it grew out of the stage of being a scientific toy, the camera and its works have been subjected to unkind comment by the practitioners of the older graphic arts. "Photographic" has been converted into a term of reproach and has been made synonymous with the unimaginative, the literal, the mechanical. But both the giving of this reproach and the meek acceptance of its damning implications by many photographers fail to take account of a very important factor in photography—*control*.

All procedures and processes concerned in photography are to a greater or lesser degree subject to control. At the outset, in working with and directing the model, there is involved control of a very subtle psychological sort. The lighting is likewise subject to control. Control of another sort is involved in setting the aperture and timing the exposure. In developing, the negative undergoes numerous chemical controls. A limited amount of personal expression is possible through the medium of the controls just mentioned, and there are many photographers who go no further, but the major opportunity for such expression comes through processing and controlled projection. The image as literally recorded on the negative is not a picture, scarcely even the beginning of a picture, but rather the potentiality of many different pictures according to the artist's comment on it in the process of printing and the attendant manipulations. Getting the image onto the negative is only taking the picture: in printing, one comes to *making* the picture.

Selection by Control.

The arts deal *selectively* with their material. The poet, the painter, the musician, the novelist—none of these is concerned with making a mere carbon copy of reality. Instead, he picks and chooses and selects from this crowded, meaningless world: and by altering, suppressing, emphasizing, he builds something that has unity and *meaning*. Such selective dealing with reality is only possible to the photographer if he avails himself of his medium's facilities for control.

Legitimate?

There are some who will dispute the photographic "legitimacy" of most of the methods and procedures hereafter described. In photography, as in other departments of life, there is an inclination to resent the ascendancy of the illegitimate over the more regularly begotten. There is a considerable group of workers with the camera, excellent technicians, self-styled "pure photographers," who declare that objective recording is the highest virtue and finest attainment of the camera, and who consequently eschew all controls except the simplest and most primitive. But the cry of "legitimacy" and "purity" is, in art, all too often the recourse and excuse of the pedantic and ineffectual. Not "Is it pure?" but "Is it beautiful?" not "Is it legitimate?" but "Does it move you?" are still the ultimate tests of picture, poem or symphony.

Growth of Projection Printing.

The present tendency of photography is toward the smaller camera. Most of the 8x10 war horses of not so many years ago have been turned out to pasture. Today a $3\frac{1}{4}$x$4\frac{1}{4}$ instrument is rated as large, while those of smaller size are growing in use and popularity. Increased precision of camera engineering, together

15

with improved emulsions and developers, have made this possible. The old contact print, except as a method of proofing, is becoming a rarity. Consequently the technique of projection printing takes on increased importance.

Imagination and the Camera.

Despite the tremendous possibilities of projection control, it is little practiced, much less understood, by the average pictorialist today. It is airily dismissed by the ignorant as "trick photography," and regarded as heretical and blasphemous by the so-called purists. Such neglect is unfortunate, for projection control offers the pictorialist with imagination a solution for his discontent with much present-day photography and its literal snap-shot ideals.

With nearly every picture—no matter how bad—there was something in the original subject that made an imaginative appeal to the person who took it. But this imaginative urge is, much of the time, betrayed by the undiscriminating and prosaic vision of the camera. The camera records all that it sees—and no more. The imagination, on the other hand, simultaneously sees much less than is there—and much more: much less, in that it disregards inconsequential details; much more, in that it emphasizes significant facts. It is rare indeed that the camera by itself can capture the essence of the subject as the photographer has seen it in his mind's eye. Through projection control, however, it is possible to isolate and develop the picture elements that made the subject originally interesting.

Three Methods.

The three general types of projection control that are herein described and illustrated are capable of wide and diverse application. Through Local Printing, Distortion, and Combination Printing one may gain greatly increased power over pictorial material. These three procedures when mastered give one control over emphatic placement, control over contours, control over local tone and contrast, control over expressive shapes and forms, and control over the dramatic association of ideas. The procedures described are not easy to apply, although they are simple in principle. But through mastery

16

of them one may greatly increase his expressive power in the photographic medium.

These three methods by no means exhaust the potentialities of projection control. Because of the relatively small amount of work being done in this new field, it is still rich in undiscovered possibilities of method and effect. It is to be hoped that this discussion of it will lead others, not only to deeper appreciation of this type of technique, but also to effort, by original experiment, to improve and extend its capacities.

Chapter Two

Equipment and Materials

In all procedures and processes of photography, simplicity is a virtue of the highest order. A clutter of equipment and a complexity of material bring photographers to untimely graves—and without any pictures to show for it. So I have made the following list of equipment and materials for projection control as brief and simple as possible.

Projection enlarger.
Orange filter.
Printing frame.
Tilting easel for frame.
Aperture board.
Black wax pencil.
Jar of "opaque."
Time clock.
Assorted masks for printing.
Print developer.
An ample supply of enlarging paper.
Other equipment incidental to normal finishing.

The negative for use in projection control should not be too large. The largest convenient size is 4x5. A negative $2\frac{1}{4}$x$3\frac{1}{4}$ or $3\frac{1}{4}$x$4\frac{1}{4}$ is easiest to work with. Contax, Leica, and other 35 mm.

negatives lend themselves admirably to the various processes of projection control, although demanding greater skill and more critical care in manipulation than those of somewhat larger size.

The Enlarger.

For use with medium sized negatives, the horizontal type of enlarger with nine inch condensers and a 400-watt bulb is found to be the most flexible sort of projection apparatus, lending itself readily to all the methods of control. My personal preference is for the old Thornton-Pickard machine, which is of English manufacture and embodies condensers of a type developed for use in aerial photography. A good lens of about 8 inch focal length (such as a Carl Zeiss or a Goerz Dagor) is essential. Such a projection outfit as this is not easy to find, but it is worth looking for.

For 35 mm. and other small negatives, a vertical type of enlarger with a lens of short focal length is preferable, as the conventional horizontal machine requires excessive space to step the small negatives up to an 11x14 area. Until recently, the only truly high precision enlargers adapted to the small negative were those manufactured by the makers of Leica and Contax. The "Precision" enlarger, lately put on the market by Eastman, is a very fine instrument, made extremely flexible by readily interchangeable lenses and condensers. The Simmons "Omegas" and the Burke and James "Solars" are also quite satisfactory.

All procedures of projection control are equally applicable to either the vertical or horizontal type of machine.

Although more critical in handling, the condenser type of enlarger is generally to be preferred to one of the diffusion type. A well-designed diffusion enlarger (such, for example, as the Elwood machine) is capable of good work, but is apt to heat up unduly.

Orange Filter.

In order to check on the progress of various projection control procedures, it is necessary to have an orange filter to protect the bromide paper against unintentional exposure. Such a filter is part

Figure 1. Printing frame tilted for elongation.

of the "standard equipment" of most modern enlargers. The filter
should be so rigged that it may be quickly and easily operated.

Printing Frame and Easel.

The printing frame should not be smaller than 11x14. Most of
the procedures of projection control are more readily accomplished
with prints of generous size. It is important that the glass be flawless.
An "optical" glass of such size is expensive, but is much to be preferred if you can afford it. The frame should be so mounted that it
may be tilted forward at least fifteen degrees (as in Figure 1), with
several intermediate adjustments. It is also useful to have the frame
capable of rotation about a vertical axis, although this adjustment is
seldom called for.

With a vertical type of enlarger, tilting adjustments are generally
made in an impromptu fashion by propping up one edge of the
frame with a book. However, the Eastman "Precision" enlarger has

Figure 2. Enlarger tilted for enlongation.   Figure 3. Aperture board used with horizontal enlarger.   Figure 4. Fingers controlling opening in aperture board.

taken care of these matters by permitting the machine itself to be tilted. (See Figure 2.)

Aperture Board.

An important accessory for local printing is the "aperture board." This device is easily made. Basically it consists simply of a piece of stiff black cardboard, about 12x14 inches, in which is cut a circular hole about an inch and a quarter in diameter, two inches above the center and two inches to one side of the center. The diameter of the opening may be altered to meet individual needs: it should be of such size as to readily admit the first two fingers of the left hand. This accessory is shown in use in Figures 3 and 4.

The home-made device described above is entirely adequate for the use to which it is put. But if you prefer something a little more dressy and tailor-made, there are several fancy versions of the "aperture board" on the market. One type offers you, by twirling a disc, a selection of holes, of various shapes and sizes. Another consists of a sort of iris diaphragm which may be manipulated into all manner of wierd contours. Either of these is almost as good as the simple piece of cardboard with the hole in it.

21

Timer.

It is frequently desirable, in projection control, to match the tone of separately printed areas. To do this accurately, some sort of timing device is required. The traditional procedure of counting chimpanzees is scarcely accurate enough for this purpose. In the absence of more ostentatious equipment, an ordinary, loud-ticking alarm clock will serve excellently. The conventional alarm clock is built so that it ticks *four times a second*. All that is necessary to keep accurate track of time is to listen to the clock, mentally accentuating every fourth tick, thus:

TICK tick tick tick TICK tick tick tick TICK tick tick tick, etc.

Guided by this pattern, you can then count your chimpanzees with complete accuracy:

NO chim-pan-zee ONE chim-pan-zee TWO . . . etc.

If you do a great deal of printing, however, you will probably find it worth while to invest in an automatic timer. There are a number of devices on the market, not too expensive, designed to turn off the enlarger light at any pre-set time from one to sixty seconds.

Printing Masks.

For fitting compositions of varying sizes and proportions into the 11x14 shape it is necessary to have a considerable number of printing masks of sundry proportions and sizes, varying from a square to a panel. The following set of eight openings would be ample to meet most needs:

10x10	10x13
10x11½	9½x13
10x12	9x13
10x12½	8½x13

The masks are made of light-weight bristol board, the openings being meticulously cut with straight-edge and razor blade. Any rough edges, or other carelessness in cutting, become very evident when the print is made.

To guard against stray reflections, it is a good idea to blacken the inner edge of the cut-out with ink.

Printing Paper.

When I stipulate an "ample supply" of paper, I mean ample. You must be prepared to have most of your prints achieve an ignominious end in the waste basket while you are learning these methods. Indeed, if you are reasonably self-critical, you will probably throw *all* of them away for quite awhile. A bromide or chlorobromide of medium weight is preferable, such as Defender "Velour Black I," Eastman "Opal," or Agfa "Brovira." For the methods outlined hereafter, a "normal" paper will serve in most cases. There is occasional use for "soft" paper, never any for "hard."

The Strength of Limitation.

One of the commonest characteristics of the photographic amateur, and one of his worst faults, is his fickleness. Instead of trying to master a unified scheme of equipment and materials, he needs must try everything once, and so embarks on an interminable series of experiments that cost money, waste time, and prove nothing. Possibly he amuses himself extremely, but beyond that his accomplishment is nil. Far better for him if he would at the outset get the best equipment he can afford and the least he can get along with, and solemnly resolve to limit himself to one kind of film, one kind of paper, and one kind of developer. The uncertainties and variable factors in photography are all too numerous as it is without exercising unholy ingenuity in inventing fresh ones.

23

Chapter Three

Negative Quality

Before there can be a print, there must be a negative. This is so obvious a fact that it should seem superfluous to mention it. But the implications of the fact are blithely ignored by many camera workers who try to make prints with any sort of negatives, exposed by guess and developed by the grace of God.

Nothing is more essential to good photography than correct negative quality. And about nothing is there more misunderstanding and wrong teaching. Photographers are still hag-ridden by that ancient fallacy "Expose for the shadows and let the high lights take care of themselves"—a fallacy going back to the Stone Age of photography when the main idea was to be sure of getting an image on the plate. This fallacy has been fostered and brought down to date by manufacturers anxious to ensure the users of their materials getting a picture of some sort—even though the negative looks like a dark day in a coal mine. Favorites of this cult of overexposure are those physics of ailing negatives—reducers and intensifiers. The inevitable running mate of overexposure is underdevelopment, an equally pernicious photographic habit which is largely encouraged nowadays by the wholesale methods of commercial workers. The requirements for negative quality that I shall set forth are not easy to meet, as there are many degrees of overexposure and only one of correct exposure. But for projection printing and all the procedures of projection control a negative of correct quality is an absolute necessity.

The Negative for Projection.

It is important at the outset to learn to recognize and distinguish such a negative. It should be brilliant, and by conventional standards slightly thin, ranging from complete transparency in the deepest shadow through a long scale of half-tones to dense black in the extreme high lights. Such a negative when examined carefully by holding it in front of an illuminated sheet of white paper shows two main divisions of tonal quality:

1. A relatively dense area.
2. A translucent area.

The denser area (which represents, of course, the lighter portions of the print) is at no point completely opaque or black save at one or two small spots which correspond to the most intense high lights of the original image. Throughout the translucent area (representing the darker passages of the print) there is a *suggestion* of drawing and a faint *tone* over it all, except in a few small accents (representing the "deepest darks"), which are clear and transparent as glass. Finally, there is, between these two dominating areas of tone, a considerable and clearly distinguishable range of half-tones. Such a negative, if held between a light globe and a white sheet of paper, will, even at a distance of six or eight inches, cast a clear image of itself.

Negatives of this peculiar type of brilliance are not to be obtained by conventional photographic practice. Indeed, the procedure which is herein advocated runs counter to many accepted ideas on exposure and development.

Four Factors.

There are four factors that determine the quality of a negative. Control of these factors will ensure a negative of proper quality for projection.

Two of these factors relate to characteristics of the subject matter itself. These are:

1. Lighting.
2. Local tone.

The importance of these two factors in determining negative quality is not generally recognized.

The other two factors relate to procedures directly affecting the negative:

3. Exposure
4. Development.

These are, of course, the traditional factors in negative processing. But the traditional understanding of these two factors (based primarily on contact printing) does not lead to the best results in producing a negative for projection.

Lighting and Local Tone.

For good negative quality, it is important that the subject matter itself should be of relatively *low contrast*. In the first place, the subject matter should contain no large areas of contrasty local tone. In the second place, it should have no extreme contrast imposed upon it by lighting.

What do we mean by "local tone"? Unless you are photographing a plaster cast, different parts of your subject matter are differently colored. For example, your model has light brown hair, blue eyes, a medium complexion, and a green dress. These various colors are translated by the camera into different local tones of gray.

Now, any subject matter that puts into opposition large areas of the extremes of local tone will not yield a good negative. Such subject matter, for example, would be a model with a pale complexion and a large mass of black hair. If you tried to get detail in the face, the hair would be empty of detail. On the other hand, detail in the hair could be secured only by sacrificing it in the face.

Photography is at its best in exploiting the gradation of the medium half-tones. Good subject matter, therefore, will furnish plenty of these. The extremes of local tone may be present, but they should appear only in very small areas. (The nature and placement of these "accents" will be explained presently.)

By means of *lighting*, various degrees of contrast may be imposed on subject matter. Even subject matter with little variation in local tone may be made extremely contrasty through wrong lighting. (See Figure 7.) For the best quality in negatives for projection, avoid heavy contrasts in lighting.

In another book* I have described a method of lighting which secures effective illumination of low contrast. In terms of the Weston exposure meter, the ratio between the shadow and light area of the face in a portrait should not exceed 1:4. If the reading for the shadow area is 6.5, for example, the light area should not read more than 25. And if the light area reads 13, the shadows should not fall below 3.2.**

Exposure and Development.

A great deal of photographic procedure has been (and still is) based on:

1. An exposure ample enough to be sure of getting an image.
2. A development brief enough to avoid blocking up the amply exposed image.

Now, as a sort of rough-and-ready way of getting an image every time you shoot, this method has its points. It is, for this reason, the procedure generally advocated to the supposedly uncritical amateur by manufacturers of photographic materials. But this method is incapable of producing a projection negative of good quality.

This method is euphemistically called "exposing for the shadows." Photographers who thus "expose for the shadows" are obliged to jerk their negatives prematurely from the developer in order to prevent the light area from blocking up completely. By so doing they cheat themselves of some of the detail in the very shadows that they exposed for. As to the light area, they get something that is printable,

---

* Pictorial Lighting, Camera Craft, 1937.

** For more about this ratio of shadow area to light area (the "S:L ratio"), see "Flash in Modern Photography" (Camera Craft, 1941), Part II, Chapter Three.

but starved for half-tones. When once the half-tones have merged themselves with the high lights, they are joined for good, and no amount of hocus-pocus with underdevelopment or reducers can ever take them apart again.

Instead, for the best quality for projection, negative procedure should be based on

1. *An exposure compatible with the light area of image.*

2. *The fullest possible development.*

1. It is entirely logical that exposure should be based on the light area of the image.* It is in this area that the principal interest lies in at least 99.9% of all photographs; so it is only reasonable that this area should be made to furnish the fullest possible photographic reward to the eye in the way of gradation and half-tones. In practical terms, "exposure based on the light area" means an exposure slightly less than normal. Very definitely, it does *not* mean underexposure.

2. For best quality, a negative so exposed should be left in the developer until development is complete—or until, in the jargon of the technicians, development has reached "gamma infinity." A negative that has been correctly exposed for the light area *cannot be overdeveloped.* Up to the moment that fogging begins there is the possibility of the development of latent detail.

This extended development may range from three-quarters of an hour to an hour and a half (or even longer) in a developer of reduced alkalinity. The combination of clipped exposure and extended development takes advantage of the period of "tolerance" (which in most modern emulsions is considerable) between the attainment of gamma infinity and the incipience of fog. With a properly timed exposure there is a period of at least half an hour during which—for all practical purposes—absolutely nothing "happens" in the emulsion after the completion of development. Development may be complete in fifteen minutes, in twenty minutes, or in

---

* Note that we say "light area," NOT high lights. High lights are the few brilliant points of extreme illumination, found usually on the tip of the nose, the chin, the catch lights in the eyes, etc. These high lights register as opaque spots on the correctly exposed negative.

three quarters of an hour; but by generously prolonging the development time, you protect yourself against variations in emulsions, slight variations in exposure, and variations in the strength of the developer.

It should be noted that some emulsions (particularly the ultrasensitive type) will not stand up to extended development. There are some developers also (particularly those heavy in alkali) that should not be so used. Here are a few films and developers that may be safely recommended under these conditions.

Films:
  Agfa Plenachrome and Finopan
  Dupont Superior
  Defender Portrait
  Eastman Verichrome
Developers:
  Borax-Metol
  Agfa D-6
  Glycin

It should be emphasized that the last two factors of this type of procedure—clipped exposure and extended development—are based on strict adherence to the first two—restricted contrast of lighting and local tone. Any attempt to apply this sort of exposure and development to contrasty lighting or subject matter will result in disaster.

A Sample of Procedure.

All theories of exposure represent an effort to fit the restricted range of half-tones of the negative to the range of tones afforded by the subject. Since the negative range is nearly always much shorter than the object range, it is obvious that some sort of compromise must be made, as it is impossible with the average subject involving local colour to record simultaneously on the same negative the full range of half-tones in the light area and complete detail in the shadows. By basing exposure on the light area, the full range of half-tones in this part of the image is reproduced on the negative with only the extreme high lights attaining full blackness. Figure 5

Figure 5
Exposed for the
light area;
balanced lighting.

is a straight print from a negative obtained under such conditions. This print immediately impresses one with its tangible, three dimensional quality. Note the nice distinction in local colour between the whites of the eyes and the light area of the flesh. Note also the range of delicate half-tones in the light area. The few high lights are crisp and brilliant, and the shadows rich and illusive. The quality of the blacks is substantial and velvety.

The older compromise, that of exposing for the shadows, represents an effort to get on to the negative everything recordable in the subject. But note what happens when a negative is exposed for the shadow area: while you are waiting for the small amount of light from the shadows to record itself, things are going wrong in the light area. The extreme high lights build up to black first of all, and, because they cannot get blacker than their ultimate black, they re-

main there while all the adjacent half-tones catch up and merge themselves with the high lights. A print from such a negative shows fine detail in the shadows, and a bleak light area bereft of all detail or gradation. Figure 6 shows the result of exposing for the shadows: the lighting is identical with that of Figure 5. Comparing Figure 6 with Figure 5 it is immediately evident that the modelling of the face has been destroyed so that it looks flat and on one plane. The distinction of local colour between the whites of the eyes and the flesh tones has been lost. The gradation of half-tones in the light area has been wiped out completely. There are no crisp high lights, and no rich blacks. The shadows are filled with wiry unpleasant detail. Compared with the rendition in Figure 5 the hair in Figure 6 looks meager and mousy.

A comparison of these two prints should make it evident that,

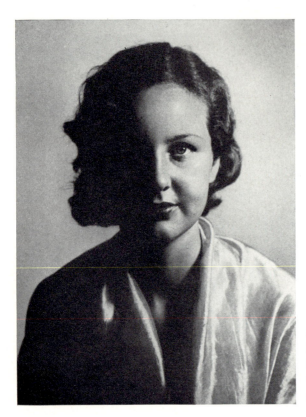

Figure 7.
Exposed for the
light area;
"modelling light"
with reflector.

aside from photographic advantages, there are very definite pictorial and psychological justifications for exposing for the light area. It is to this part of the picture that the eye goes first in search of subjective or thematic interest. Hence this part should reward the questing eye with fine detail, delicate gradation and subtle modelling—the qualities which constitute photography's unique contribution to pictorial art. In the shadows, on the other hand, illusion should prevail, and too much literal detail there is a distraction and an annoyance.

It must always be borne in mind that this procedure is postulated on lighting and local tone of *low contrast*. Figure 5, for instance, is a typical example of the so-called Basic Light.*

* Pictorial Lighting, Chapter Three.

32

Figure 8.
Exposed for the
shadows;
"modelling light"
with reflector.

A contrasty lighting, or the typical studio "modelling light" with reflector, results, when one exposes for the light area, in complete loss of the shadow area. Figure 7 is a fair example of what happens when one attempts to combine this method of exposure with the "modelling light." The exposure in this case was the same as that used in Figure 5. Note that the shadow area is completely blacked out, although ample detail was evident to the eye at the time of taking the picture. Observe, however, that in the light half of the face, on which the exposure was based, there is just as fine gradation and modelling as in Figure 5. Obviously, this method of exposure cannot be applied to pictures taken in direct sunlight, which is contrasty in the extreme. But in the shade, or under a cloudy sky, one may successfully base exposure on the light area.

In Figure 8 is demonstrated the conventional portrait procedure, which seeks to secure a three dimensional effect through the use of a "modelling light" instead of through delicate gradation of half-tones. The lighting is the same as in Figure 7, with exposure based on the shadow area. Notice that the light area is blasted and burnt out just as it was in Figure 6. Only in the shadow area does any modelling survive.

No effort has been made to exaggerate the differences between these four prints. They received identical treatment in the dark-room. All four were printed for the same length of time on the same kind of paper, and were developed for the same period in the same developer.

Appearance of Negative.

Aside from procedure, how may we recognize this paragon of negatives? We have already, in a general way, indicated the appearance of a projection negative. Let us now note more particu-larly its rendition of half-tones.

Check prospective projection negatives in front of an illuminated white background. Note carefully the relative areas occupied by the different half-tones. The diagrams in Figure 9 will be of help in placing the quality of the negative. Figure 9A shows an all-too-fami-liar type of tone distribution. It is characteristic of most record shots and of all attempts to deal with contrasty subject matter or lighting. Note that most of the area is given over to the extremes of the tonal scale, and that such gradation as remains is crowded into a small and restricted area. Such a negative as this is altogether hopeless for projection.

Figure 9B shows the tonal distribution of the so-called "brilliant" negative. Here more opportunity is given to display the gradations of the middle tones, but the extreme tones still occupy too large an area. This type of negative has some pictorial uses, but is not the best for projection control. The relatively large area occupied by the extreme tones reveals that the accents of intense light and shadows are to a considerable extent lost in the surrounding area. Note also that in types A and B the lightest area is somewhat veiled

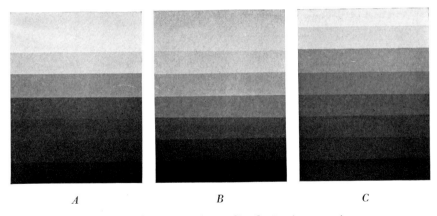

A   B   C

Figure 9. Three types of tone distribution in a negative.

over: this means that the extreme range of tone represented by clear glass is not taken advantage of, thus losing accent blacks in the print.

In Figure 9C is shown the tonal distribution that should be sought for in a projection negative. Here we have the fullest possible extension of the range of the middle tones. A small amount of dense black remains as the high-light accents. And there is the added range of clear glass (in the shadow accents).

Accents and Their Placement.

These "accents" in a good projection negative are small and crisp. The high-light accents represent complete, or nearly complete, reflection of the illumination. They occur naturally at the points on curved surfaces nearest the light source. The shadow accents, on the other hand, represent the portions of the image at which there is complete, or nearly complete, absorption of the light. They are frequently adjacent and complementary to corresponding high lights.

In a negative of the quality shown in Figure 9C, a face illuminated by the Basic Light (as in Figure 5) would probably show these accents at the following points:

<blockquote>
High-light accents—
The eyeball (one accent in each eye).
The teeth.
</blockquote>

The finger nails.

Jewelry.

Highest sheen of blond hair.

Portions of rounded flesh nearest source of illumination.

Shadow accents—

Pupil of eye.

In cornea immediately below upper lid.

Spots in nostrils.

Upper corners of upper lip.

Small openings between strands of hair.

Other *small clean* shadows throughout image.

The customary position of these accents is shown in diagrammatic fashion in Figures 10 and 11. In order to show the accents clearly, their effect is of course greatly exaggerated.

A projection negative of the quality shown in Figure 9C gives, with effective placement of these accents, an effect of vitality, crispness and sparkle that cannot otherwise be obtained in photography. The precious elements of black and white, instead of being squandered in huge empty shadows and in bleak expanses of overexposure, become bits of condiment that lend zest to the whole.*

Other Negative Requirements.

Correct quality is, of course, the primary requisite of negatives for projection. However, there are a few other attributes advisable in a negative that is to be subjected to projection control. These may be listed briefly.

1. The negative should be small . . . Any size larger than 4x5 is difficult to handle.

2. The principal object in the negative should be fairly well centered, with ample neutral space on all sides. This arrangement allows for adjustment and manipulation.

3. If the negative is to be used for combination printing, the background should be opaque. That is, a Semi-Silhouette

---

* For additional discussion of negative quality and of exposure and development practice, see Pictorial Lighting (Camera Craft) and Mortensen on the Negative (Simon and Schuster).

Figure 10. Placement of high-light accents.   *Figure 11. Placement of shadow accents.*

Light should have been used in photographing the subject.

Summary.

This discussion of negative quality has covered a good deal of ground. Let me summarize the principal points:

1. The subject matter should be of low contrast, both in lighting and in local tone.
2. The negative should receive an exposure compatible with the range of half-tones in the light-area of the image proper.
3. It should be given an extended development, ranging from three quarters of an hour to an hour and a half in a developer of reduced alkalinity.
4. The negative should be translucent and brilliant, never heavy.
5. It should contain a full range of half-tones.
6. It should contain a few definitely marked accents of full black and complete transparency.

Chapter Four

Basic Projection Printing

The modern trend toward the smaller camera gives increased importance to the technique of projection printing. This technique is learned by the majority of photographers, as I myself learned it, by bitter experience: only by much wasteful fumbling do they find their way to clean, certain and expeditious methods. While an awkward period is inevitable in the learning of any technique, be it playing the piano or digging post holes, this period can be much shortened and much precious time and material saved by starting right. The amateur should as early as possible devote himself to acquiring manual skill and strive to reduce his dark-room procedure to a ritualized routine.

Even supposedly advanced students of photography that I have met have had difficulty with simple projection printing. And until one is capable of making a good clean bromide print, it is perfectly futile to talk of projection control. Hence this chapter.

Handling the Enlarger.

We have already mentioned the necessity of a really *good* enlarger —preferably of the condenser type. But like a good camera, or a good horse, the good enlarger requires careful handling. The condenser type of machine is much more critical and sensitive than any other. Every flaw, every finger mark, every wandering speck of dust is meticulously recorded, and nothing but arduous "spotting" can

"Balkan"   *William Mortensen*

make good the carelessness that let them be there.

There are two ways of allowing for focusing adjustments on a horizontal projector. One way, which is probably the commoner, provides for the movement of the focusing board while the projector remains stationary. The other method has the focusing board fixed, except for tilting adjustments, while the projector slides to and fro. The latter solution is the one that I prefer. The slightly greater effort needed to move the heavy projector is offset by several advantages. All the focusing adjustments are made with the machine, instead of being divided between the machine and the board. The latter arrangement also obviates the considerable danger of spoiling the focus in removing or replacing the printing frame.

Before printing, make sure that all glasses are immaculately clean—the printing frame, the negative carrier, the projector lens, and the condensers. Watch especially for specks of dust or lint on the condensers, for such specks will cost you many tedious hours of "spotting." The negative, likewise, should be carefully dusted and examined for finger marks. These, if found, should be removed with a little alcohol on a wad of cotton. In projectors of the horizontal type there is danger of the lamp being displaced from the center of its housing. If this happens it produces an unequal distribution of light. Check for this frequently by closing the lens down to its last stop, when any unevenness of illumination may be clearly detected.

A Note on Diffusion.

If you are the owner of any diffusion discs, please dust them carefully and drop them in the nearest sewer. Any occasional problems that may arise with wiry negatives can be met with slight adjustments of focus. But habitually to debauch good clean negatives into an accumulation of wooly blotches is the worst of photographic crimes, and any one who indulges in it may justly be suspected of having concurrent talents for rape and mayhem.

Focusing.

Focus the enlarger always with the lens wide open. Determine the sharpness of the focus by watching some small detail (in portraits the high light in the eye is usually chosen) near the center of the picture. If you can find no such crisply defined detail, you may be reasonably certain that your negative is not worth printing.

When the focus is as sharp as you can possibly get it, close down the lens aperture by at least two stops. This serves to eliminate any remaining discrepancy in focus, such, for example, as might be caused by slight buckling of the negative in the carrier. If any considerable amount of projection control is to be used, however, the aperture should be closed down almost all the way. By this means the printing operation is slowed down so that manipulations may be carried out in a reasonably deliberate manner.

Working at such reduced apertures stresses the need for cleanliness, since under these conditions every speck or smudge on the condensers is brought into sharp definition.

Care of Materials.

The same sort of cleanliness and care must be observed in handling materials. Developing trays should be stored away from dust and be well rinsed both before and after using. Decent cleanliness in storing and handling chemicals is much more important than picayunish accuracy in measuring and weighing them.

Use fresh developer every time you print. It is the poorest of economies to try to make yesterday's developer do for today. And check the hypo frequently. Of all photographic chemicals, hypo is the cheapest. What ever you may save by nursing along last month's hypo, you pay for ten times over in spoiled or inferior prints.

Choice of Paper.

Photographers who try to make prints from all sorts of negatives of all types of subject matter are compelled to pay a great deal of attention to fitting the scale of the printing paper to the scale of the negative. Thus a short scale (or "flat") negative requires a short scale (or "contrast") paper in order to secure the best rendition of all half-tones. And a long scale (or contrasty) negative calls for a long scale (or "soft") paper. In order to deal satisfactorily with negatives of all types, one needs to have on hand paper of at least three degrees of contrast, and preferably four or five.

However, if you can depend on getting a negative of fairly uniform characteristics, most of this complication may be eliminated. The procedure outlined in the preceding chapter, if carefully carried out, will yield such a negative. If this procedure is followed in all details, you need to have only two grades of paper—normal and soft. Most of the time, in fact, you will need only normal.

I have elsewhere* discussed the matter of paper surfaces. If you are genuinely interested in pictures for their own sake, you will not be seriously tempted by such non-pictorial issues as conspicuous surfaces and exotic colors.

A choice of the following papers is suggested:
> Brovira 7051 (soft)
> Cykora 2 (normal)
> Defender I 2 (normal)
> Defender D 2 (normal)
> Kodalure G (normal)
> Agfa or Eastman Projection Proof (normal)

It is a good idea to use the Projection Proof, whenever possible, for tests and experiments, particularly while you are learning printing procedures. It is substantially cheaper than the other papers.

Development Time.

It may seem illogical to discuss development before exposure, but it really is not. Exposure must be based on pre-determined correct development.

The emulsion on paper is thin, considerably thinner than the emulsion on film. *Complete* development is therefore required. Every print must be developed to "gamma infinity." Up to the point that fogging sets in, a print is capable of picking up more half-tones, more pungent blacks in the accents.

---

* Print Finishing, Part One, Chapter One.

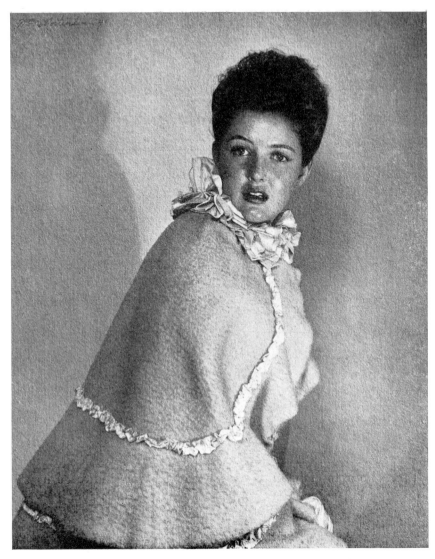

"Girl with Cape"   *William Mortensen*

This gives us a lead on determining the proper development time for a printing paper. We want to develop the paper fully, and yet stop comfortably short of fogging. For practical purposes, we may say that *the proper development time for a paper is four-fifths of the fogging time.*

We may thus determine the proper developing time for any given paper in any given developer: Put a scrap of the paper into the developer and note how long it takes to fog. Four-fifths of this time will be the indicated developing time—for *that* paper in *that* developer. Shield it from the safe-light during the test, so as to exclude the possibility of light fog. Take your time from the first perceptible trace of gray in the emulsion. This will be a very pale tint, and in order to detect it under the safe-light, it will be necessary to bend the paper back and compare the color of the emulsion with that of the wrong side of the paper.

If the paper fogs in five minutes, the indicated developing time is four minutes. If it holds out for ten minutes before fogging, the development time is eight minutes. In all cases, the development time thus determined will be considerably longer than the time generally advocated by the manufacturer. The manufacturer's recommendations are usually based on commercial rather than pictorial needs, and are concerned with turning out snappy prints in the shortest possible time. Conventional recommendations for papers generally run from one and a half to three minutes developing time. Four to eight minutes is the usual time indicated by the fogging test.

Exposure.

We have established, by means of the fogging test, the time that will give the paper the maximum development. Now we must determine the exposure that will permit of such development. Obviously, in view of the extended development, this exposure will be somewhat shorter than that usually given.

There are, on the market, numerous ingenious meters for determining negative contrasts and print exposures. However, a good many people who have tried these devices have gone back to the old-fashioned test strip as being on the whole more convenient and fully as accurate. A test strip, used consistently and intelligently, will tell you all that you need know about your negative quality and print exposure.

Making the Test Strip.

The test strip should be made, of course, with the image focussed to the same size, and with the lens closed down to the same aperture, that you propose to use in making your final print. Put the strip—which, for an 11x14 print, should not be less than an inch and a half wide—in the printing frame and so adjust it that the test is made of both the light and dark areas of the object of principal interest. In a portrait, this object would, of course, be the face.

For consistent results, the successive exposures given the strip should constitute a *geometric series.** Under these conditions, there is equal separation between successive exposures. The following series is suggested as a useful one for test strips:

4, 6, 8, 11, 16, 22, 32, 45, 64.

It will be noted that in this series the time doubles with every other exposure.

Have your loud ticking alarm clock or other timing device ready. Before you start, cover the near end of the strip with a card so that you will have an unexposed area for comparison. Now turn on your light and start counting. At the count of "4", move the card up about half an inch. Move it again at 6, at 8, at 11, and so on.

When you have completed the 64 second exposure, turn off the light and develop the strip. Give the full development as indicated by the fogging test. After the strip is developed and fixed, examine it carefully and determine which area gives the best rendition of values and the fullest half-tones. The time for this area is, of course, the proper exposure for the print.**

---

* "Geometric" as distinguished from "arithmetic." A typical arithmetic series would be 8, 12, 16, 20, 24 . . . . 48, 52, 56, etc., in which each exposure is four seconds longer than its predecessor. This would produce wide separation between the short exposures, and practically none between the longer ones.

** The labor of making test strips may be considerably reduced by the use of a "step wedge" of some sort. A special form of step wedge is furnished in the Eastman "projection print scale." Before you rely on it, a step wedge should be checked by careful comparison with regularly made test strips.

If there is any question of choice between two or three different exposures, make a second test covering this particular ground with a more closely spaced sequence of exposures. Pick the necessary sequence from the following series:

8, 9½, 11, 13, 16, 19, 22, 26, 32, 38, 45, 52, 64.

In this series the time doubles with every fourth exposure.

For purposes of projection control, the exposure should not be too short, since deliberation is needed for the various manipulations. If the indicated exposure is any shorter than 16 seconds, use a smaller aperture. If the smallest available aperture still gives too short an exposure, it will be necessary to use increased enlargement or else install a less powerful lamp in the projector.

Your final print, of course, should be exposed and developed according to findings of the tests. These tests may seem unduly tedious, but they will ensure you good and consistent results. Increasing experience will enable you to abbreviate the tests. Two or three trials will clearly indicate the developing time, so that you will not need to run another fogging test unless you change your paper or developer. Experience will also enable you to judge the exposure within a fairly close range. Then your test strip will need to cover only this range.

Developing Procedure.

In putting the exposed print into the developing tray, slide it into the solution edgeways. This movement automatically clears the emulsion of aid bubbles. Never put the whole hand into the developer. If the print is clipped pincer-wise between the first two fingers of the right hand it is never necessary to dampen more than the tips of these two fingers. The developing tray must never be placed directly under the safe light, as extended development under these conditions will undoubtedly produce light fog. The imminence of fogging is detected by turning back a corner of the print and comparing the tone of the plain side of the paper with that of the unexposed margin of the emulsion. If the latter shows the slightest tincture of grayness, the print should be pulled immediately.

Fixing.

Before going into the hypo the print should be briefly rinsed in an acid short stop bath* If many prints are being made, this rinsing is necessary to prevent rapid depletion of the hypo; but it is advisable in all cases, as hypo tends to flatten the half-tones of a print that is not cleared of surface developer. Residual developer is also apt to produce yellow to brown stains on the print. After the print is in the hypo, resist for five minutes the temptation to turn up the lights and examine it. Even when a print appears well fixed, it is still susceptible to fog and loss of contrast. Let it remain in the hypo for twenty minutes and then rinse in running water for one hour.

Drying and Finishing.

Before drying the print, swab it carefully with a soft, clean cloth. Some meticulous operators have recommended drying frames covered with linen. I believe that this is an unnecessary refinement, as I have for many years without mishap dried my prints on frames covered with galvanized chicken wire. Before it is bone dry a print should be straight-edged and pressed.**

Now we come to a point that touches on personal and professional pride. No print is fit to appear in society until it has been dried, straight-edged, pressed, spotted, trimmed and mounted. And yet we encounter amateurs and occasional professionals with so little sense of decency that they will exhibit, to public or friends, blotchy prints with curled corners and ruffled edges. A photographer should no more think of making such a disillusioning display than an actress would think of showing her public what she looks like when she wakes up in the morning.

The Two Basic Faults.

In the last twenty years I have seen a lot of photographs made by students. From examining their work, I have concluded that, in

---

* Since acetic acid is no longer generally available the following substitutes may be used in the proportions indicated: 2 ounces of citric acid to 1 gallon of water; or 4 ounces of Sodium Bisulfite to 1 gallon of water; or one part of 45 grain white vinegar to two parts of water. For a detailed discussion of this matter see American Photography for April 1942.

** Full detail on these procedures will be found in Print Finishing, Camera Craft, 1938.

prints, there are just two technical faults that are really fundamental: *flatness* and *extreme contrast*.

Oddly enough, the students as a rule paid little attention to these faults but were greatly distressed by lesser failings. "What makes that stain?" said they, "Why am I not in focus?" or "What causes those white specks?" These are things of small account, relatively, and may be corrected by a little tactful instruction in common care and cleanliness; but the faults are fundamental and their causes are often hard to arrive at.

There are several possible causes for both these faults. It is important to know them all.

A flat, grimy, grey print may be caused by—

1. A negative that has been overexposed and subsequently under or overdeveloped.
2. Old or inferior film.
3. Vitiated negative developer.
4. Overexposure and underdevelopment of the print.
5. Print developer too soft or depleted.
6. Light-struck or over-age paper.

A too contrasty print lacking half-tones may be caused by—

1. A too contrasty negative emulsion.
2. Too contrasty lighting of the subject.
3. Too contrasty local colour in the subject.
4. Too hard a negative developer.
5. Too hard a print developer.
6. Too vigorous a printing paper.

The Ultimate Photographic Test.

The two ultimate *photographic* tests of a print are DEFINITION and GRADATION. The definition test dictates that all edges must be sharp, that all parts of the image must be in focus, and that there must be no fuzziness or falling off. The gradation test dictates that there must be the fullest possible photographic presentation of the half-tones of the subject. No negative is adaptable to the uses of projection control unless it is first capable of making a good, clean straight print.

"Cloth Merchant—Scotland"   *William Mortensen*

Chapter Five

Local Printing

The camera is unselective.

This is a truism—trite, hackneyed and obvious. But it can't be said too often to anyone who is trying to make the best use of his camera. What *you* see and what your *camera* sees are two different things. You see, for the most part, what you want to see; you see a thing in the aspect that interests you, plus various emotional garnishings peculiar only to yourself. But the camera sees a subject stolidly and complete. It records the whole works, not only the single aspect that pleases you, but a whole collection of trashy and distracting incidentals that you overlooked entirely. Indeed, sometimes it seems that it perversely *invents* disagreeable details.

One of the first things that the photographer must learn to do is to put himself in the camera's place, as it were, and to see things as it sees them. But, despite our best efforts, it still happens that we get many things in our pictures that we wish were not there, and leave out things that we thought we saw in the subject. Somehow, the wrong things are emphasized, shadows fall in the wrong places, and tonalities are wrongly balanced.

In correcting these faults of emphasis and balance, the several procedures of *local printing* are extremely useful.

The Scope of Local Printing.

Between the lens of the enlarger and the focusing board there is a space varying from a few inches to several feet. By manipulations within this neglected space, directing and regulating the passage of the light, are performed the various operations of local printing.

Local printing lends itself to emphasis of significant and salient details (significant and salient to you, that is, although your camera may not see it that way). Certain essential or climactic points, such as the eyes in a portrait, often demand darkening in tone. And local printing, by deftly placed accents, may effectively stress the key contours in a composition. In this placing of accents, in the "losing and finding of outlines," photography comes about as close as possible to the concise quality of draughtsmanship.

Conversely, local printing aids in the elimination of subordination of detail that is unpleasant, superfluous or incongruous. Unfortunate shadows under the chin or on backgrounds, confused masses of extraneous detail in backgrounds or in clothing, accidentally included objects that are meaningless or in direct conflict with the essential idea of the picture—these and similar problems may be often solved by local printing.

By dodging—which is a variety of local printing—the placing of contrast may be regulated. This is frequently advantageous, for negatives often fail to comply with the axiom of picture construction that the point of greatest interest and the point of greatest contrast should coincide.

What the Camera Sees.

We have already mentioned the camera's embarassing facility in painstakingly recording trivialities and carefully emphasizing the wrong things. Let us look at a specific instance.

In Figure 12, we were attracted by the delicate blonde beauty of the child. But look at the variety of irrelevant and disturbing items that the camera managed to include:

    1. The pattern of the dress is very conspicuous and "busy".

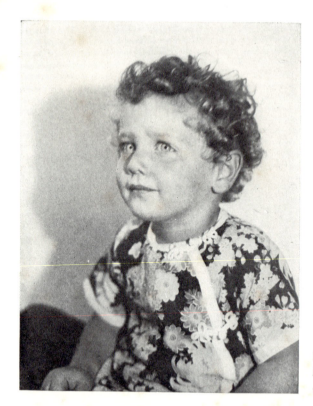

Figure 12.
Straight print,
without control.

2. There is a shadow on the background.
3. There is a large, dark, out-of-focus lump of nothing-in-particular in the lower left corner.
4. The eyes are too pale.
5. The hair is too dark.
6. The ear is too conspicuous.
7. The nostrils are too heavily shadowed.
8. The nose shadow is too strongly marked.
9. Shadows on the neck and around the mouth are dark and smudgy.

All of these things are definitely at variance with the qualities that attracted us to the subject matter.

52

Figure 13.
Spot printed, dodged,
and vignetted.

A Sample of Procedure.

Figure 13 comes much nearer to the picture we wanted to get. The difference between Figures 12 and 13 is a matter of selective local printing. This is the general procedure:

With the orange filter in position, frame the head to the placement and relative size that you wish. Close down the diaphragm of the lens to stop f.22. With the right hand hold the aperture board (described in Chapter Two) in front of the lens, between it and the printing frame. By masking the hole with the fingers of the left hand it is possible to cut the light passing through to a crescent or a mere pin-point. (See Figures 3 and 4.) Note that a replica of the image appears on the aperture board — slightly blurred and indistinct it is true, but sufficiently definite to guide you in your printing. Now remove the filter and let a small round spot of light play over one of the eyes. Do likewise to the other eye, being very careful to give equal time to each. (For results of unbalanced printing see Figure 49.) Then allow the light to play over the lips for about the same length of time, taking care to avoid the nostrils. Next paint in the hair bordering both sides of the face and darken one or two other accents in the hair. Now, with the hole narrowed down to a mere slit, trace down the side of the head, allowing the light to emphasize the delicate line of forehead, temple and lower cheek. Draw in the neck-line with a slight accent here and there.

Now withdraw the fingers from the hole and move the aperture board nearer the lens until the entire head* is seen on the print. Allow a general exposure of about the same length as that given each of the eyes, gradually bringing the board near the lens until the entire negative has had an exposure. Replace the orange filter, remove the negative from the enlarger, and close down the lens to its smallest stop. Then, with your fist clenched and held in front of the lens, remove the filter and, with the shadow of your fist shielding the face of the image, revolve your arm and elbow, keeping the center of the print from being exposed. (See Figure 14.) Work gradually nearer the lens until you have obscured the entire print. Replace the filter.

In the finished print, Figure 13, it is apparent that the errors listed above have been corrected. The various distracting and irrelevant items have been elided or eliminated, and the attention has been focused on the few simple and significant elements.

The Tools for Local Printing.

Before discussing further the methods of local printing, let us check up on the tools available for the purpose.

1. The "aperture board"—described in Chapter Two.
2. The "local dodger," consisting of a tuft of cotton (Figure 14B) or a bit of passe-partout attached to a wire handle.

---

* If the hair is quite dark, give a preliminary exposure to the face only before moving the aperture board to include the hair.

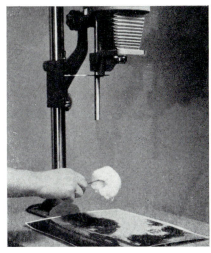

Figure 14-A. Dodging with fist.   *Figure 14-B. Dodging with tuft of cotton.*

3. Specialized devices, usually consisting of cut-outs, made for individual problems.

More useful and versatile than any of these, however, are two other gadgets—your hands. For dodging a large area, such as the head in a portrait, the fist is generally used. (Figure 14A.) For smaller areas, the finger tip is better. For straight-edged areas at the sides of pictures, the flat of the hand is used. The hand can frequently be shaped to special contours, or may even take the place of the aperture board.

Three Types of Local Printing.

The procedure outlined above, in connection with Figure 13, involves three different types of local printing.

1. Spot printing.
2. Dodging.
3. Vignetting.

The first two—spot printing and dodging—are complementary processes. Spot printing consists in limiting the printing action to

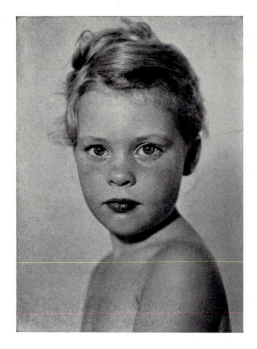

Figure 15.
Straight print, without control.

a small chosen area. Dodging (which we might call "local *not*-printing") consists in eliminating or reducing the printing action in a chosen area. As a matter of fact both operations always take place *together;* since we spot-print by means of dodging out everything else, and we dodge by printing all other areas. This statement may seem a bit cryptic, but use of the processes will make it clear.

The third type of local printing—vignetting—is really a specialized sort of spot printing for large areas.

Now let us consider the separate types of local printing in more detail.

Spot Printing.

Spot printing consists, as we have said, in limiting the printing action of the negative to a small area of image. This is usually done by interposing the aperture board so that only a small beam is projected onto the sensitized paper. The diameter of the printing beam may be increased or lessened by moving the board closer to or

56

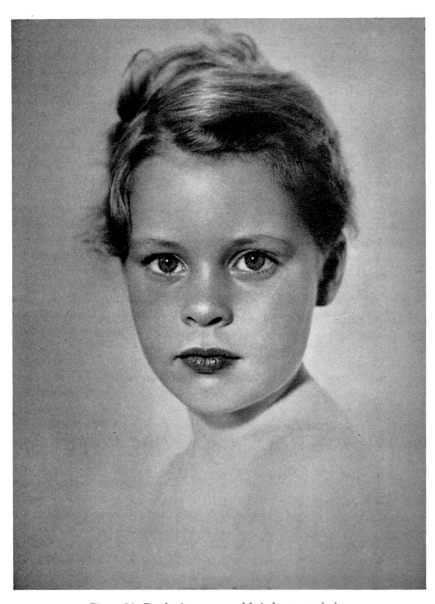

Figure 16. Emphasis to eyes and hair by spot printing.

farther from the lens. Further control of the shape and size of the beam is obtained by inserting one or more fingers through the aperture in the board. On some occasions the hand alone may be used instead of the board. By combining this procedure with a general printing it is possible to print some areas more strongly than others.

In practically all cases of spot printing there is also *some* general printing of the entire image. However, the relative amounts of spot and general printing will vary greatly in different cases. Roughly, we may notice three categories of this relationship:

1. The general printing is *very light*, only enough to indicate the main contours. Almost the entire effect is created by the spot printing. (This was the procedure followed in Figure 13.)
2. The image is printed up *almost* to normal density. Then spot printing is used to give additional emphasis to chosen points. (This was the procedure in Figure 16, in which the eyes received the extra accent.)
3. The main image receives *full exposure*. Then spot printing is used to darken obtrusive white areas.

The last two methods are apt to prove most generally useful. Not only is the first method extremely difficult in execution, but it demands very special subject matter—delicate, impersonal, and high in key.

Spot Printing for Emphasis.

Spot printing is generally used for one of three purposes:
1. Emphasis.
2. Elimination.
3. Balance.

First, the matter of emphasis. Portraits are frequently improved by accents of additional printing of certain salient features. The eyes, lips, and the shadows in the hair are the spots most likely to need such treatment. Figure 13 is a rather extreme example of it.

Figures 15 and 16 show that this emphasis may lend a certain

Figure 17. Typical snapshot material.   Figure 18. Disturbing elements eliminated
by spot printing.

distinction to an otherwise commonplace bit of portraiture. Note
how the darks in eyes and hair, although they appear black in Figure
15, are made (in Figure 16) to appear even blacker and are given
an increased pungency by slightly "holding back" the surrounding
areas. The aperture board was, of course, used for this purpose.

Use this sort of emphasis sparingly. The whole value of the
added accents is lost if they are scattered liberally throughout the
picture.

Spot Printing for Elimination.

In pictures such as Figure 13, in which the general printing is
slight, the period of spot printing will accomplish the elimination
of various undesirable details. Thus, in Figure 13, the heavy shadow
under the chin, the shadow on the background, and the contrasty
pattern of the dress are all eliminated by the simple device of avoid-
ing them while spot printing.

Such complete elimination as this, however, can only be accom-

Figure 19. Straight print, without control.   *Figure 20. Finished portrait with balanced tones.*

plished when, as in Figure 13, the general printing is very light. In cases in which the general printing is normal, or nearly so, elimination or reduction of such detail as the hat shadow in Figure 29, can only be brought about by dodging.

Figure 17 shows conditions commonly met in run-of-the-mill snapshots—out-of-focus background and disturbing detail in the doorway alongside of the head. Figure 18 is no masterpiece of portraiture, but local printing and reframing have made it a much more pleasing piece of work.

Spot Printing for Balance.

Another use of spot printing is in the *balance of tones.* There are numerous common predicaments (particularly in portraiture) in which such balancing is called for.

1. *Balancing two heads in one portrait.* A frequent problem of the photographer nowadays is the making of a presentable portrait

Figure 21. Straight print, without control. *Figure 22. Finished portrait with hair tone balanced.*

of mother and daughter in which daughter is sun-tanned to the ultimate degree and mother has her customary indoor complexion. Ordinarily, with a negative of this combination, if you print for a good presentation of the daughter's face, mother will be anaemic and underexposed; while if you print to give mother's complexion a break, daughter will look like an African princess.

The same problem appears, in a less aggravated form, whenever a blonde and brunette are photographed together. It is also apt to occur whenever a man and woman are photographed on the same negative. (Figure 19.)

The reasonable and practicable solution of this predicament lies in local printing. In fact, it is the *only* solution, as such extensive retouching is quite out of the question. Figure 20 shows how the situation in Figure 19 may be corrected. The delicate half-tones of the paler face are first allowed to imprint themselves through the aperture board up to nearly the required density. Then the entire

Figure 23.
Fogged by light leakage.

picture is exposed until the other face is properly printed. This procedure (provided the two operations are correctly timed) will secure a more pleasing balance between the tones of the two faces.

2. *Balancing within the limits of a single face.* Very dark hair combines with a pale complexion to present a common photographic dilemma. As indicated above, both elements cannot be advantageously rendered at the same time (even on soft paper): either the hair is excessively black and devoid of gradation (Figure 21) or else the face is under-printed. By means of local printing with the aperture board it is possible to hold back somewhat the dark area of the hair and at the same time to secure a stronger rendering of the flesh tones. (Figure 22.) In this case, a preliminary exposure was given to the face only. A second briefer exposure was given to the face and hair together. Finally, the shoulders were vignetted

62

Figure 24. Fog corrected by spot printing.

by moving the aperture board slowly toward the lens until the entire picture was exposed.

Sunburn creates another situation that calls for balancing. A woman usually hides her ears under her bathing cap when she goes in swimming and thus keeps them in a state of pristine pinkness, while the rest of her face assumes various tints of terra cotta. This problem also is solved by means of the aperture board, which administers additional printing to the reluctant ears.

Balancing is also called for when aggressive and distracting notes of white are present—such, for example, as a handkerchief in a coat pocket. Such areas may be subdued by spot printing.

A fairly common condition that calls for spot printing grows out of careless handling of lighting units. Unless you check your lighting frequently, you are very apt to get pictures in which the background is noticeably darker on one side than on the other, or a unit placed too close may give you a "hot spot" on the background. Such faults may be readily corrected by slight additional printing in these areas.

Figure 23 shows another rather common technical mishap. Careless handling of film resulted in light fog in the upper right hand corner. Local printing in Figure 24 restored the tone to this area and also recovered the cloud, which failed to print in Figure 23.

Local Printing by Cut-Outs.

Ordinarily the aperture board is the only tool needed for spot printing. Occasionally, however, it is desirable to limit the printing to more precise contours. In such a case it is necessary to use a cut-out.

It is *possible* to make a cut-out by projecting your negative on a piece of light bristol board and tracing the desired contour with a pencil. But this method is not very satisfactory: in spite of all efforts, you get in your own light; and the proper contour is often hard to recognize in the negative form.

It is much better to do the thing properly by making a full-size preliminary print (preferably on double weight paper). The cut-out made from this is bound to be accurate.

Figure 25.
The two parts of a cut-out.

There will, of course, be two parts to the cut-out. (Figure 25.) Part "1" includes the principal subject; part "2," the background. "2" is used for spot printing; "1," as we will see in a moment, for dodging.

Cut-outs are also used sometimes in Combination Printing (as will be described in Chapter Seven).

Figure 27 shows the results obtained by the use of a cut-out to secure additional emphasis in a figure in a landscape. The "2" cut-out was used for part of the exposure time to hold back the background, which in Figure 26 is too nearly the same tonality as the figure.

Dodging.

Dodging is in effect the reverse of spot printing, since it consists in holding back the print in chosen areas. This is done by casting a restraining shadow on the sensitized paper during projection. In practice all sorts of instruments are employed in dodging—the tip of the finger, the fist, the flat of the hand, a wisp of cotton on a wire handle, a peacock feather, a cut-out, or any other implement that the emergency and its inspiration may suggest. The choice of the instrument depends upon the size, shape, and location of the area affected.

According to the demands of the situation, two different procedures are followed in dodging:

1. Dodging during printing, with the negative in the enlarger.
2. Dodging after printing is completed, with the negative removed from the enlarger.

The first procedure is followed when small and limited areas are affected; the second, when alteration of tone or reduction of contrast is desired over a large area of the picture.

Three Uses of Dodging.

There are three general uses of dodging.

1. *Correcting unbalanced illumination.* Carelessness or reckless experimentation with your lighting is liable to produce the all-too-familiar effect of a face strongly lighted on one side and lost in shadow on the other. Or you may get a shadow from an overhanging hat without providing for adequate reflection in the dark area. Of course, it is much preferable to get your lighting correct in the first place; but, in order to salvage an otherwise good negative, and to avoid the inconvenience of a re-sitting, it is sometimes useful to resort to dodging. By holding back the shadow area during printing (with the finger tip or a bit of cotton on a wire), you may not only correct the gross unbalance in the lighting, but may actually pull up into visibility detail and half-tones that were apparently lacking in the lighter areas. (See Figures 28 and 29, also Figures 30 and 31.)

This unbalance is characteristic of uncontrolled lighting, particularly of daylight when there is no diffusion from high fog or thin clouds. Most pictures taken by direct sunlight require some such

Figure 26. Straight print, without control.   *Figure 27. Emphasis on figure by spot printing with cut-out.*

correction of balance. Figure 32 is a rather extreme case, since most of the subject and background are in shadow, with the principal illumination falling on such secondary items as the edge of the face and the weeds in the foreground. In addition there is a distracting reflected glare on the white skirt. The correction (Figure 33) is made by means of spot printing and dodging. The whole picture is first given a brief preliminary exposure—just enough for the detail in the background. The figure then is given additional printing, with the aperture board protecting the background from additional darkening. Finally, the whole upper three-quarters of the picture is shadowed out with the flat of the hand, giving additional exposure to the pale vegetation in the foreground.

Flash photography provides another application of dodging. Illumination from the flash bulb is very intense and, when you are working at close quarters, falls off very rapidly. Consequently, any foreground in your picture, any object nearer the camera than your principal subject matter, is practically certain to be burnt up on

Figure 28.
Straight print,
without control.

the negative. This local overexposure may be effectively corrected by dodging, and an appearance, at least, of half-tones may be restored to the foreground.

Dodging may also be used to correct some lesser faults in lighting, such as a dark corner in a background. A shadow on the background, as in Figure 12, either may be directly dodged out with a tuft of cotton, or it may be simply elided in spot printing—which was the actual procedure in this case.

2. *Adjusting tonal relationships with the background.* When a Semi-Silhouette lighting is used,* it sometimes happens that there is too violent a contrast between the tone of the face and the tone of the background. This condition may be corrected by dodging. After the face is properly printed, the negative is removed from

* Pictorial Lighting, Chapter Five.

"Francois Villon"   William Mortensen

Figure 29. Hat shadow reduced by dodging.

Figure 30. Straight print, without control.   *Figure 31. Window detail recovered by dodging.*

the enlarger, and, with the constantly moving shadow of the fist shielding the area occupied by the face, the background is given additional exposure. This procedure puts a little tone in the blank white background and produces a much more pleasing relationship between it and the face.

In Figure 34 the strong contrast between the dark costume and the brightly lighted background detracts from the presentation of the face. Heavy dodging of the background, as in Figure 35, shifts the principal contrast, which now lies between costume and face, and makes a better picture.

3. *"Dodging in" for emphasis.* A slightly different procedure is that known as "dodging in." This is done, as described above, with the negative removed from the enlarger. But in this case the fist is held somewhat nearer the lens and is gradually moved in until its shadow covers the entire printing surface. This procedure protects from alteration both the central image and the immediately

70

Figure 32. Straight print, without control.

Figure 33. Unbalanced lighting corrected by dodging and spot printing.

Figure 34. Straight print.

Figure 35. Relationship to background adjusted by dodging.

Figure 36. Straight print, without control.

adjacent background, causes an almost imperceptible darkening of the corners of the picture. Added emphasis is thus given to the image, since the attention is held comfortably within the picture area and prevented from straying into the corners. Increased "dodging in" of a portrait produces an effect of strong illumination opposite the head. Abuse of the procedure results in unpleasant and freakish "halo" effects.

Dodging with Cut-Outs.

Dodging is generally done with rather informal tools—the fist,

Figure 37. Background fogged by dodging (with cut-out) with negative removed.

a finger tip, or a tuft of cotton. But occasional cases require more precise workmanship. It is then necessary to use a cut-out.

In Figure 36, for example, which was shot in a second-hand shop, the background is completely irrelevant. Instead of eliminating the background by spot printing—a possible procedure—we decided simply to fog it until it became inconspicuous and unrecognizable. (Figure 37.) A cut-out was needed to protect the complicated contour of the principal image.

First, an exposure was given for the entire picture. Then, with the orange filter in place, the cut-out was adjusted to exactly fit the image. Finally, the negative was removed and an additional exposure given to the background area, darkening it and reducing its contrast.

Dodging in Landscape.

The examples thus far have been largely in the field of portraiture. But dodging also has numerous valuable uses in landscape.

By means of dodging, tone may be restored to a sky that is blank and devoid of gradation. Figure 38, for example, was made on a brilliant gray day, and the original print shows a blank, white area where the sky should be. Not even a heavy filter would secure tone in the sky under these circumstances. But an excellent tone was produced by dodging. After an exposure sufficient to print the foreground, the right hand was held so as to shadow the picture as high as the skyline, while the left forefinger shadowed the figure where it is silhouetted against the sky. The sky area was then given additional exposure, the right hand being gradually moved higher and nearer the camera until the entire picture was shadowed. The method gives a sky with gradation, pale near the horizon, darkening toward the zenith.

Figure 40 demonstrates how progressive dodging may be used to bring out negative detail, latent but ordinarily unavailable. The straight print, Figure 39, shows a nearly opaque shadow in the foreground and a sky devoid of clouds. In making the controlled print, the exposure time was divided into three approximately equal periods. The first period consisted of a straight exposure, without dodging. Then, for the second period, the hand was held so as to shield the foreground shadow. Finally, the hand was raised and brought nearer the lens, so that for the third period nothing but the dense sky was exposed. The finished print, Figure 40, discovers clouds in the sky and a satisfying amount of detail in the shadow. Figure 40 is undoubtedly much nearer to what the eye reported than is Figure 39.

Dodging may introduce atmospheric interest into otherwise commonplace landscape material. The arresting quality of Figure 41 is due almost entirely to the dramatic streak of light. This effect was introduced by dodging during printing. The rather grim and con-

"Country Lane"   *Alex Lilburn*

Figure 38. Sky tone added by dodging.

Figure 39. Straight print, without control.

Figure 40. Detail recovered in sky and foreground shadow by progressive dodging.

Figure 41. Dramatic effect enhanced by dodging.

fused prospect in Figure 42 is pointed up by the added accent of the setting sun, introduced in making the finished print, Figure 43. The forefinger was held so that the shadow of its tip fell where the brightest spot on the horizon was to be. During the exposure, the finger was rotated in a semi-circle about this point.

Vignetting.

The third species of local printing is the process known as "vignetting." Those of sufficient maturity to recall that heroic age when cameras were cameras and photographers had hair on their chests may remember a gadget known as a "vignetter," consisting of jagged semi-circle of cardboard attached to the facade of the 8 x 10 instrument. This produced an effect of head and shoulders floating unattached in mid-air, which in those times was considered quite the

Figure 42.
Straight print,
without control.

last word. An analogous effect may be produced in projection printing by means of the aperture board. An exposure is first made of the face (assuming you are dealing with a portrait negative), then the board is gradually moved nearer the lens of the enlarger, giving progressively diminished exposure to the surrounding parts of the print. This yields a picture pale and underexposed at the edges, deepening to its darkest tones at the center. The general effect is thus the reverse of that obtained by "dodging in," and as a means of emphasis is not so successful as the latter process, owing to the distracting high key of the edges and corners. However, vignetting may be combined with "dodging in" to very good advantage: the falling off of image is supported by the darker tones secured by dodging, and the two effects unite to give powerful dominance to the center of the picture.

"*Winter Evening*"   *William Mortensen*

Figure 43. Glow added by local dodging.

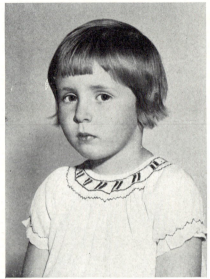
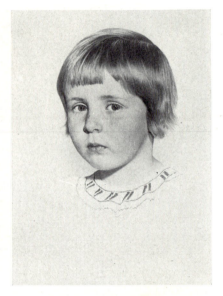

Figure 44. Straight print.   *Figure 45. Vignetted only.*

The effect of the various processes may be judged from Figures 44, 45 and 46. Figure 44 is the straight print, without control. In Figure 45 the head is merely vignetted. Note that the line of the shoulder and detail of the dress fades out, letting the head hover in a state of equivocal non-support. Figure 46 is both vignetted and "dodged in." The head is here supported by the darker tones in the corners, and given greater pictorial dominance than in Figures 44 or 45.

The Technique of Local Printing.

Up to this point we have devoted considerable space to discussion of *what* can be done with the various types of local printing, but have passed lightly over the practical problem of *how* it is done. The manipulations involved in local printing are simple enough in principle, but are annoyingly difficult in performance. They require dexterity and experience and may be learned only by doing, not by reading about them.

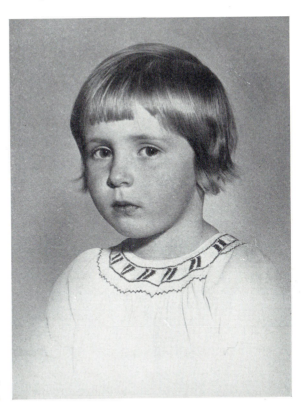

Figure 46.
Vignetted and dodged in.

However, a few practical suggestions may be offered which may serve to shorten the painful and disillusioning period of apprenticeship.

1. The various tools used in local printing—the aperture board, the tuft of cotton, the fist, etc.—must be kept in gentle and *continuous* motion while in use. If the tool stops moving at any point, the printed area will have a sharp contour instead of a softly gradated edge. The aperture board should be vibrated constantly, or kept moving in tiny circles. In dodging in, the fist is held so that its shadow remains in the central area of the picture, while the forearm and elbow, swinging from the shoulder, rotate about it. When a cut-out is used, it means that a

well-marked contour is desired; so the movement should be very slight, just enough to barely fringe the edge of the printed area.

2. Work always with the projector lens at a small aperture. You will thus be able to proceed deliberately and arrive at more accurate results. A miscalculation of one second would not count for much if your total exposure was thirty seconds, while it might be very serious if your total exposure was only four seconds.

3. The essence of local printing is accurate timing. Matched areas (such as the eyes) must receive matched exposures. Close attention must be paid to the relationship between the exposure of the general printing and the exposure of the spot printing. They must always, and in all areas, add up to the *correct* exposure.

4. You must keep your wits about you when you are doing local printing. You must at all times have a clear mental picture of what you have done and what you are going to do next. Otherwise, you may very easily skip one area and print another one twice. If you discover yourself getting rattled, slip in the orange filter immediately and pause until you figure things out.

5. Rehearse each picture before you print it; feel out the sequence of operations and plan the timing. And when you print it, do it as you rehearsed it, without inspirational variations.

6. The several sorts of local printing must be thought of simply as methods for controlling *tone*. If you try to go further and attempt to effect *structural alteration* by this means, you overstep the proper limits of the process and are inviting trouble.

7. I think that I may be safe in promising you that your first print using these methods will not be a masterpiece. But study the thing anyway and try to figure out what went wrong. And then immediately plan, rehearse and

"Midday"   *William Mortensen*

Figure 47. Reduction of shadow on face by dodging.
Glare on beach darkened by spot printing.

Figure 48. Straight print.

Figure 49. A typical early attempt at local printing, showing bruises and inequalities.

execute another print. And then another. And then another. . . . By the time you reach the first gross, you may note some improvement.

8. Since you are undoubtedly going to use up a lot of printing paper, don't squander *expensive* material on your awkward period. Practice instead with the low-priced "Projection Proof." And, if you should accidentally happen to turn out a good print, this paper will finish very satisfactorily.

For Instance.

Figure 48 represents the sort of problem that you might undertake in your first trials at local printing. The negative is good, and it makes a good clean projection print. However, there is a little too much detail in the dress, and the lighting is a little too contrasty. The rather cross-hatched arrangement of shadows keeps the eyes from dominating the picture as they should. There is too much loss

84

Figure 50.
Correctly spot printed,
vignetted, and dodged in.

of detail in the shadowed portions of the hair. Finally, there is unequal illumination of the background.

In Figure 49 an effort has been made to deal with these matters by means of dodging and spot printing. However, both the general printing and the subsequent spot printing have been insufficient, so that the final print is pale and anaemic. The dark area in the hair has been held back too much, so that it is actually lighter than the rest. The eyes are unequally printed, and absent-minded handling of the aperture board has allowed several bruises to develop.

Figure 50 shows a reasonable solution of these problems. Vignetting has reduced the amount of crass detail in the dress. The hair tone has been more pleasingly balanced, and reduction of the shadows in the face permits the eyes to dominate. The background has been equalized and dodged in to darken the corners slightly.

Chapter Six

Distortion

All art is distortion.

Not the copying of reality, but the interpretation of its meanings in terms of a medium, is the business of art. This means clarification by selective emphasis and elimination, it means the personal comment of the artist—all of which means distortion. Every art involves distortions dictated by the conditions of its particular medium—be it paint, sounds or words. Even the most literally conceived and executed photograph involves distortions: colours reduced to a scale of grays and solids to a convention of a single plane.

Under the broad interpretation of the term, all the procedures of projection control are simply methods of distortion. But the particular distortion that I have reference to in this chapter is the *distortion of form.*

For some reason, the distortion of form is, beyond all other sorts of distortion in art, most bitterly resented by the Philistine, who likes to think that literal duplication and likeness are the whole concern of art. He likes to see a nice recognizable cow (complete with brown and white spots) in a recognizable field (complete with daisies) in front of a recognizable sunset. But when Picasso paints the cow, or Redon paints the daisies, or Turner paints the sunset, he sneers and writes letters to the newspapers about the crazy Modernists.

The Background of Distortion.

As a matter of fact, distortion of form is, of course, far from being a modern practice. The Assyrians, the Egyptians, the Doric Greeks, each race had its characteristic and distinguishing distortion. Even the Venus of Melos, popularly cited as an instance of perfection of form, distorts to a considerable degree the normal proportions of the human body.*

Every culture expresses itself in terms of its particular distortion. There is cruelty and incisiveness in the lines of Assyrian carving. Chinese art forms seem to develop out of, and to return to, the circle and the sphere, which well summarize the balanced and self-contained characteristics of the race. In the dizzy lift of Gothic cathedrals and in the strangely attenuated sculptures that hang aloft, one reads of an age that raised itself above this dusty existence to one of mystic exaltation. In modern American cities the vertical thrust of sky-scrapers speaks of indominable growth, and on the prairies the heavy horizontals of Frank Lloyd Wright's houses tell of the vast extension and spaciousness of the American scene.

Indeed the instinct to distortion is deeply imbedded in the primitive stratum of every human being. Young children, who have an artistic instinct that they usually grow out of or have educated out of them, have a great zest for "tall tales," and are prone to make this dull world more interesting by means of effective exaggeration. The small becomes infinitesimal, and the large, gigantic, as they report it, and the dark end of the upper hall becomes interestingly populated with lions and bears. Closely akin to these products of the child-artist is the legend of our Northwest, that characteristically American contribution to folklore, that tells of the exploits of Paul Bunyan and his blue ox, Babe.

Instead of being a sign of aesthetic degeneracy, as angry Academicians are apt to imply, the present day fondness for exaggerated forms is a welcome sign of return to primitive first principles that

---

* The average figure is about six and a half heads tall; but Venus is eight heads tall—a relationship which makes her practically a pinhead by so-called normal standards.

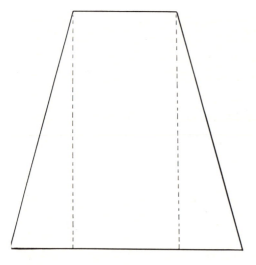

Figure 51.
Shape of image elongated by tilting frame.

recognized (as the child instinctively does) that the business of a work of art is to make an effect, *not to report a fact.*

The Photographic Use of Distortion.

Through the photographic use of distortion one escapes further than is possible by local printing from the literal, realistic conditions of the negative. It is the most effective and most drastic expression of the emotional grasp of form. It is for this reason more limited in its applications. One must be very sure that the distortion is already suggested or implied by lines or forms in the original image. If there is, further, a hint of the bizarre, the symbolic, or the idealized, distortion may probably be resorted to with excellent effect. Such distortion may be slight—just a sly underlining of latent tendencies of line or mass—or it may be extreme and startling. In any case, be sure that the distorted form is more significant than the original. In putting the principle of distortion to use, don't look for subjects that could *possibly* be distorted, but look for those that *demand* to be distorted.

Various things have motivated the distortions used in the illustrations for this chapter. Figures 54 and 56 might be designated as idealizations, in which there is a pointing up of exaggerations

Figure 52.
Elongation of inverted
image.

already implied in the originals. Figure 58 belongs rather to the field of the symbolic, in which the distorted form has distinct emotional value. In Figures 66 and 67, the distortion partakes of the quality of caricature or cartoon. And the corrective distortion employed in Figures 61 and 63 is entirely utilitarian in intent.

Methods.

Elongation is the type of distortion most commonly employed in projection control. Such elongation as that employed in Figure 54 or 56 is obtained by tilting forward the printing frame. (See Figure 1.) The angle of the tilt determines the amount of distortion produced.

When the printing frame is placed at an angle, of course most of the image is thrown out of focus. This condition is met, however, by closing down the diaphragm of the enlarger lens to almost the

Figure 53.
Straight print.

smallest stop. When this is done, it is possible to bring all parts of the image into focus, despite their differing distances from the lens. Before closing down, obtain a sharp focus at about the *middle* of the image. It will not be necessary to close down so far, in this case, as it would be if the focus were secured at either the top or the bottom.

In printing with a frame tilted forward at the top, your oblong image takes on about the shape shown in Figure 51. In order to be able to trim the picture back into shape, it is necessary that the image on the negative have ample neutral space surrounding it.

Since a pyramidal formation is generally desirable in a picture, the type of elongation shown in Figure 51 is usually followed, with the top of the image narrowed and the bottom widened. However,

90

Figure 54.
"Circe."
Finished print with elongation,
spot printing, and dodging in.

there is occasional use for the opposite type of distortion, produced either by inverting the negative or by tilting the frame *backward* at the top. Figure 52 illustrates this variation.

Samples of Procedure.

This is the procedure followed in making Figures 54 and 56: Tip the printing frame forward about fifteen degrees. (See Figure 1.) Frame the head, being careful to keep the line of the features perpendicular. With the lens wide open, focus the image at the center of the face. (It may be noted in passing that slightly different distortions may be obtained by focusing at the top or the bottom of the image.) Now close down the diaphragm to nearly its lowest stop, or until the top and bottom parts of the picture become

91

Figure 55.
Straight print.

sharp. Give an exposure, which will, of course, owing to the small lens aperture, be considerably longer than normal. Spot printing may be employed also if you wish. After the exposure has been made, replace the printing frame in its usual vertical position, and with the negative removed from the enlarger and the lens closed down, "dodge in" as described in the previous chapter.

In elongations of this type, it is necessary that the subject be very formally arranged, with the line of the features vertical and the shoulders level. Otherwise, asymmetrical distortions will be produced.

"Fear" (Figure 58) is a combination of several procedures: local printing, elongation, and multiple printing. A straight print of the original negative shows the extent of the manipulations.

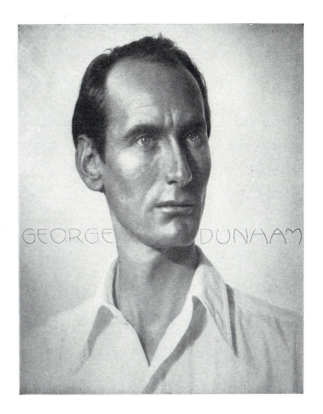

GEORGE DUNHAM

Figure 56.
"Portrait"
Finished print with
elongation.

(Figure 57.) The printing frame is tilted and the negative focused upon it, as above described, taking care to allow space in the background for the addition of the graduated shadows. After closing down the lens until the entire image is in focus, an exposure is made, employing spot printing to emphasize the dark shroud around the head, and to build up the contrast near the center of the picture. Vignette by moving the cardboard nearer the lens until the whole image has been exposed. Replace the orange filter and rack the enlarger back about an inch. This will of course produce a slightly larger image. With the fist so held as to protect the image already exposed, remove the filter and expose again, allowing only the dark edge of the drape and bit of the diaphanous gauze to record themselves. Replace the filter and repeat the process, moving the enlarger

Figure 57.
Straight print.

further back each time for three or four exposures. Let each exposure be a little less than the one before, thereby securing the mysterious gradation of shadow-forms in the background. Finally, remove the negative, close down the diaphragm to its lowest stop, and do the usual "dodging in."

Distortion in Landscape.

Distortion is a device that may be effectively employed in landscape also. Since there usually is in landscape no immediately recognizable basis of comparison, distortion is not so apparent as in a picture involving the human element. Yet it may serve the same end, giving additional stress to the effective formations in the picture.

In Figure 59, for example, the picture gains its principal effectiveness through the receding planes of the hills. These planes have

"Fear"   William Mortensen

Figure 58. Finished print with elongation, spot printing,
multiple printing and dodging in.

"Evening"   F. F. Lockwood

Figure 59. Distortion applied to landscape, emphasizing receding planes of hills.

been emphasized by elongation, which has stretched the low-lying hills into lofty ranges.

Everyday Uses of Elongation.

All the examples of distortion that we have thus far cited belong to the category of the exaggerated and stylized. However, the procedures described in this chapter also have their more normal and pedestrian applications.

Aside from its pictorial uses, elongation is sometimes a valuable device in ordinary portrait work. A face that is noticeably round or broad may be more flatteringly presented if a *slight* amount of distortion is employed. The elongation should never be enough to be detected. For this purpose, the printing frame is tilted only slightly, usually not more than five degrees. Figures 60 and 61 illustrate this application of elongation. To prevent the distortion from becoming apparent, it is necessary, as in Figure 60, that the head be erect and the shoulders level.

A common photographic fault is that shown in Figure 62. Unless

Figure 60. Straight print.   *Figure 61. Portrait with slight elongation.*

Figure 62. Architectural distortion.   *Figure 63. Distortion corrected by counter-distortion during printing.*

Figure 64.
Straight print.

your camera has a rising front, it is impossible to avoid such converging lines when dealing with tall architectural subjects. However, the distorted perspective of Figure 62 may be corrected by counter-distortion in printing. The angle of the tilting frame is adjusted until the converging lines of the image on the negative are exactly neutralized by the diverging lines of the projected image. (Figure 63.) If the frame tilts forward only, it will be necessary to project the image upside down in order to make this correction.

Lateral Distortion.

If the printing frame or negative carrier is so arranged that it may be rotated about a vertical axis, it is possible to secure distortion in a lateral direction. This type of distortion is less generally applicable than elongation, but may be occasionally used to produce very

"*The Incubus*"   *William Mortensen*

Figure 65. Use of lateral distortion.

Figure 66.
"Uncontrolled Projection"
Use of local distortion.

strange results. In Figure 65, the negative was somewhat tilted, so that the principal elongation took place along the diagonal.

Local Distortion.

In the foregoing examples the whole picture is subjected to equal distortion. It is possible, however, to elongate a portion of the image while the rest is rendered normally. Such local distortion is best suited to caricature in a humorous or satiric vein. To accomplish this sort of distortion a piece of white bristol board, 11x14, is substituted for the printing frame. Thumb-tack the bottom and curl

"Abrasion-Tone!"   *R. P. Piperoux*

Figure 67. Use of local distortion.

the upper half forward. With the lens wide open, focus the image on the curved portion; then close down till all parts of the image are sharp. Fit the bromide paper to the curve, clipping it along the edges to hold it in correct alignment. In exposure, allow for the reduced aperture. This method of distortion admits of endless variations: the field of distortion may be placed wherever wished, and the degree and direction of the distortion controlled with fair accuracy. As in other phases of projection control the opportunity is large for individual development and application of the basic principle.

Figures 66 and 67 are examples of this type of procedure. Figure 67 is a former pupil's portrait of himself after a large evening spent with "Abrasion-Tone."

Chapter Seven

Combination Printing

Among the earliest elaborations on the simple photographic process were trials at combining parts of several negatives into a single print. Two of the best known of these early examples of combination printing are Henry Peach Robinson's *Fading Away*, based on three negatives, and Rejlander's *The Two Ways of Life*, a fabulously elaborate allegorical piece incorporating parts of (believe it or not) thirty negatives.*

Now, without going into any such virtuosity as this (which is rarely worth the trouble it involves), there are numerous occasions on which the reasonably skilled photographer will find combination printing both interesting and advantageous. For the most part, in this chapter, we will stress the simpler and more usable applications of the procedure.

Two Types of Combination Printing.

Before discussing the technique of combination printing, we should note that there are two ways in which it may be used. The mechanical problems of the two types are substantially the same; the principal difference is one of *purpose*. Here are the two sorts of combination printing:

---

* These two pictures are reproduced in Photography 1839-1937, Museum of Modern Art, New York.

Figure 68. Straight print: foreground.

1. Construction in terms of *literal picture elements*.
2. Montage—or construction in terms of *ideas*.

The two classic examples mentioned above—*Fading Away* and *The Two Ways of Life*—are instances of combination printing in terms of literal picture elements. So also are Figures 79 and 87. The commonest application of this sort of combination printing is the addition of backgrounds.

The other type of combination printing is the one generally known as "montage." This term was originally applied by the French pioneers in the motion picture industry to the mere mechanical operations of cutting and assembling the various shots constituting a motion picture. It soon came to mean, however, the *effect* produced by the combination of these separate pictorial units. The term "montage," whether applied to motion pictures or still pictures, means *building up and reinforcing an idea by the combination or juxtaposition of diverse pictorial elements*. The idea may grow out of the likeness of the elements or be generated by the clash of opposites. Always in montage there is the overtone of an *idea* that

Figure 69.
Straight print: background.

is not present in the picture elements themselves, but results from their combination. In Figure 70, for instance, the strange hauteur of all cats is commented upon in terms of the inscrutability of the mask and of the ancient mystery of the pyramids.

Montage: A Sample of Procedure.

We will discuss the mechanics of montage first because it offers fewer technical difficulties than combination printing in terms of literal picture elements.

"*La Chatte,*" Figure 70, will serve to illustrate the mechanical procedure of most montages. Note the characteristics of the two original negatives, Figures 68 and 69. There characteristics are essential for negatives that are to be used in combination in the manner described:

    1.   The subjects should be photographed with a plain white background.

"*La Chatte*"   *William Mortensen*

Figure 70. Montage with additional spot printing and dodging in.

    2. The lighting of both should be either Basic or Semi-
       Silhouette in quality.*

It is barely possible, perhaps, to use negatives of a different type,
but the problem is much simpler if these limitations are observed.

    Place the negative of the principal subject (in this case the cat,
Figure 68) in the enlarger and give it a normal exposure with slight
additional emphasis to the head by means of local printing. Adjust
the orange filter to prevent further exposure, and with a wax pencil
indicate on the glass of the printing frame the key points in outline
of the subject. (In the present case it would be necessary to show
simply the side of the head and the contour of back and flank.) Now
substitute the second negative, adjusting it to its proper relationship

---

* Pictorial Lighting, Chapters Three and Five.

Figure 71. Straight print: foreground.   *Figure 72. Finished print with added sky background.*

to the first image by means of the guide marks. Note (by means of the same guide marks) whether any part of the second image *overlaps* the first. (In the present case, overlapping would be apparent with the bottom line of the pyramid and the heavy shadow in front of the shoulder.) Determine experimentally how it will be necessary to hold your hand to protect the first image. Now erase the pencil marks, place your hand so as to shadow the first image, remove the filter, and give an exposure about half the length of the first one. This gives an impression of another lighter-toned plane and permits the cat to dominate the composition. For the final step, remove the negative, close the diaphragm all the way down, and "dodge in" slightly to darken the corners of the picture and blend the two images.

This picture may be taken as a fairly typical instance of montage procedure. Let us sum up the significant points.

    1. There are generally only two negatives involved.

    2. One negative is principal subject, the other is background.

"Summer, 1931"   *William Mortensen*

Figure 73. Montage in a group portrait.

Figure 74. Straight print: foreground.

3. The two are related to each other symbolically rather than literally.
4. Both were made with Basic or Semi-Silhouette light in front of a white background.
5. The principal subject is framed and printed first. The opaque background keeps the surrounding area clean for printing the second negative.
6. A "cut-out" is rarely used for protecting the first image during the printing of the second negative. Since there is no *literal* connection between the two, it is better to roughly dodge out the first image.
7. The second negative is ordinarily printed much lighter than the first. This subordinates it and emphasizes its non-literal quality.

Figure 75. Finished print with added sky. Some dodging to emphasize light streak near center of picture.

8. Dodging in with the negative removed will further sub-ordinate the background.

Montage in Portraiture.

Montage finds an interesting application in portraiture. By this means it is possible to include in the picture a decorative and entertaining reference to the subject's hobby or vocation. Thus, if the subject happens to be a musician, the background may contain a shadowy reference to a piano keyboard, the scroll of a violin, or merely a musical staff. As in the case noted above, the decorative, symbolic element must be printed much lighter than the principal subject.

The group portrait shown in Figure 73 is an example of this use

109

of montage. This picture commemorates a summer that these six companions spent at the beach, swimming and sailing. As in Figure 70, both the component negatives were shot in front of white background. The ship, of course, was a model. Note that the background is printed faint and shadowy, and that it is dodged out an ample distance from the heads. This establishes it frankly as an unrealistic, decorative element.

Combination of Literal Elements.

The other type of combination printing is carried out in terms of *literal picture elements.* This type is usually more difficult than montage since it involves accurate and realistic matching of parts of two or more negatives.

The most common application of this sort of combination printing is the addition of backgrounds. Particularly in landscapes is this procedure valuable. A good many shots may be improved by the addition of clouds to blank sky areas.

The addition of clouds is a fairly simple matter if a few conditions are observed.

1. The original sky should be blank and almost white. A dark "filtered" sky will not work.
2. The areas immediately surrounding the sky should be fairly dark in tone.
3. The cloud negative should not be too contrasty or heavily filtered.

Under these conditions it is possible to print in a sky background without recourse to cutouts. In Figure 72, for example, the foreground (Figure 71) was printed first, with some dodging to pick up detail in the foliage at the right. Then, with the orange filter in place, the general contour of the masses enclosing the sky area were marked with the wax pencil. By the use of these guide lines, the cloud negative (Figure 80) was properly adjusted and aligned. Then the lines were rubbed out and an exposure given for the clouds. If the masses adjacent to the sky area are dark in tone (as in the foliage masses on either side of Figure 71), there is no possibility of the

Figure 76. Straight print: foreground.   *Figure 77. Finished print with added sky. Also dodging in dense shadow under roof.*

cloud image overlapping. Since the horizon line is lighter in tone, however, it was protected, during the second printing, by the edge of the hand. If a small amount of overlapping *does* appear in these cases, it may be readily eliminated by a little abrasion.*

Further examples are shown in Figures 75 and 77.

Figure 79 is a similar problem. In this case, the composition is given additional "punch" and drama by dodging out the light area in the peak of the roof.

Sky backgrounds may also be added to pictures taken in the studio. It is necessary under these circumstances, as we have noted before, that the subject be photographed in front of a well-illuminated white background.

Figure 82 is an example of this procedure. The sky (Figure 80) is from the same negative as that used in Figure 72. For the record, it may be mentioned that the figure was originally photographed standing upright. As in previous cases, the foreground figure (Figure 81) was exposed first. Then, with the aid of temporary

* Print Finishing, Chapter Four. Camera Craft, 1938.

Figure 78. Straight print: foreground.

guide lines, the sky background was fitted into position. When this was done, it became apparent that dark areas in the clouds would overlap light areas in the figure. To prevent this, the whole central zone of the clouds was dodged out with the fist during printing. A little extra dodging with the negative removed was done to secure additional contrast around the head.

A somewhat more difficult problem in combination printing is involved in Figure 85. Since it is necessary to fit the background neatly and realistically around the head, a cut-out must be used. As we have noted in Chapter Five, a cut-out is best made by cutting up a preliminary print of the precise size that the final one is to be. (Figure 25.)

The following procedure is one that is much more conveniently and accurately carried out with a vertical type of enlarger. Lay the

Figure 79. Finished print with added sky. Dodging used to lighten area in peak of roof.

cut-out of the head ("1" Figure 25) on the printing frame. Then adjust and focus the enlarger so that the projected image precisely fits the cut-out. Remove the cut-out and expose. Then, with the orange filter in place, replace the cut-out in exact register with the image. Remove the negative of the head and put in the one of the tapestry. Adjust the latter negative to the proper scale, being very careful not to move the cut-out. With the cut-out still in place, expose the second negative.

Numerous variations in effect are possible in making such a print. Here are a few.

    1. The background may be printed either light or dark.

    2. If the background seems too aggressive and full of detail, it may be thrown slightly out of focus. (Figure 88.)

113

Figure 80. Straight print: background.

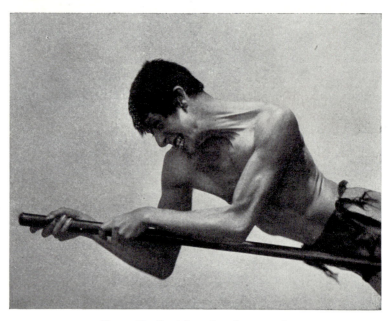

Figure 81. Straight print: foreground.

114

Figure 82. Finished combination print, with additional spot printing and dodging.

3. With the negative removed, the print may be slightly or heavily dodged in. This procedure is useful if the background is too contrasty.

It is preferable, as we have said, that the subject be photographed in front of a white background with a Semi-Silhouette lighting, as in Figure 80. However, by use of *two* cut-outs, it is possible to eliminate one background and replace it with another. This procedure, needless to say, is considerably more difficult than the one just described.

In outline, the method is as follows. You have two cut-outs as shown in Figure 25: cut out "1," of the head or principal figure, and its counterpart "2," of the background. Fit the two cut-outs together

115

Figure 83. Straight print: background.   Figure 84. Straight print: foreground.

and lay them over the printing frame. Adjust the enlarger so that the projected image of the head precisely fits the cut-out. Without disturbing "2," remove cut-out "1" and expose. Fit "1" back into place and remove "2." Adjust negative of background and expose.

This is a difficult procedure and requires precise workmanship. It should be noted, however, that slight discrepancies in the registration of head and background may usually be cleared up by use of Abrasion-Tone.

An Extreme Instance.

Figure 87 is included as an extreme instance of combination printing, representing the most intricate problem that one is likely to undertake. It illustrates the ability of combination printing to suggest spaces and properties wholly unavailable to the average amateur who wishes to experiment with complicated arrangements.

116

Figure 85. Combination print made with use of cut-out. Additional spot printing and dodging.

Figure 86. Component negatives for Figure 87.

The composition was planned by means of a sketch. The position of the elements being thereby established, a separation of the groups was made in such a way as to accommodate the facilities of the studio in space and material. Five negatives (Figure 86) were needed to accomplish this. It will be immediately noted from the accompanying reproductions that the relative size of the original images is considerably altered in the finished work. The necessary readjustments of proportion were, of course, made in the process of projection. Such portions of the negatives as fall behind other objects in the finished composition were opaqued out. Opaquing will be noted on the negative of the standing monk, as well as on the

"The Tribunal"   *William Mortensen*

Figure 87. A complicated job of combination printing.

Figure 88.

Combination of same elements as Figure 85, with background thrown slightly out of focus.

lower part of the legs of the man who is pulling the rope. The picture was printed in the natural order of receding planes, as numbered on the cut. The first negative was given the longest exposure, producing a near-silhouette. The three negatives making up the middle distance received a normal exposure, while the last one, of the large wheel, was allowed barely to record itself.

Note that, with the occasional use of "opaquing" and with a white background throughout, it was possible to make this print without employing cut-outs.

Chapter Eight

It's Up to You

For the last seven chapters I have dealt with the problems and methods of Projection Control. Now, rather tardily, I come to the much more imposing problem of controlling the photographer when he starts controlling projection.

Unhappily, there is no known method of teaching taste, good sense and discretion. To such of my readers as lack these valuable qualities this book will merely discover new ways of making bad pictures. There is no escaping this fact—nor the pictures either, for I shall doubtless be blamed for them. Babies will be butchered and ingenues outraged in the name of Projection Control.

Relevance to material must always guide the application of projection control. The control must be integral to the picture, and not a mere flourish or fancy finish. To distort a baby's head, and to locally print its eyes black and bleary, and to convert its mouth into an unsightly bruise, would seem an outrage on the most rudimentary sense of fitness—yet I have seen the thing done.

A good negative correctly lighted, correctly exposed, and correctly developed, is an absolute prerequisite. To attempt projection control with a negative of other quality than that defined in Chapter Three is sheer foolishness and can only result in the loss of time and materials. Of course, if you are starting out on a perverse hunt for trouble, you can *try* anything ridiculous—such as combination printing with a negative lacking an opaque background, or local printing with a dense negative, or a thin negative, or a contrasty negative, or a fuzzy negative; but please don't suggest that projection control is in any way responsible for the indubitably dreadful results.

Projection control must not and cannot be used to cover up earlier incompetence or carelessness. Let nothing that was said in Chapter One about the lesser importance of "picture taking" be construed as sanctioning anything but the most careful procedure at *all* stages of photographic work. Indeed, far from being a means of covering up or condoning technical incompetence, projection control is itself a delicate and precise technique. The procedures described in the foregoing chapters may sound simple, but in the first trials they will prove extremely awkward and difficult. Until the requisite manual skill is acquired don't look for any great results. And don't rush before the public, or even your admiring friends, with the early fruits of your experiments with projection control. Go about acquiring the new skill in a patient and systematic manner: instead of making twenty messes from twenty negatives, make twenty prints from one negative, trying in each to correct the recognized mistakes in its predecessors. At this stage it is not well to count too much the cost or to be niggardly of supplies. Be prepared to spoil, or rather to dedicate to educational purposes, plenty of printing paper.

Only through painful experiment and discovery may one evade the trammels of the merely technical aspects of the photographer's craft. Beyond technique lies the field of personal expression through purposeful and selective dealing with material. While it is characteristic of the artist to love the purely sensuous qualities of the world, the multitudinous textures of surfaces, the strange shapes of things—the simple recording of these for their own sake, the mere literal representation of them, does not constitute art. Intimate studies of a cart wheel, a cabbage, or a compound fracture—though they may be exceedingly fascinating and useful in affording valuable problems in composition, in exploring the possibilities of form relationship, and in revealing new fields of pattern and design—must ultimately fail of appeal because of their negligible emotional content. Human emotion has been the basic material of all great art in the past, and always will be, though each generation will express it through its own forms and patterns.

Here is an outline of procedure. Its application is up to you.